DuckDB:
Dealing with JSON Data

Djoni Darmawikarta

Table of Contents

Introduction

Welcome to **DuckDB: Dealing with JSON Data.**

DuckDB database has a rich set of JSON functions.

It is a practical book, every one of the functions is clarified and demonstrated by examples.

If you want to learn how DuckDB handles JSON data, this is the book of choice.

Prerequisites

To learn the most from the book, please try the examples. All you need is a DuckDB database with its CLI client and the JSON Extension, all of which come with the installation.

If you never use DuckDB with CLI, Appendix A will get you initiated.

You will need to be familiar SQL (Structured Query Language). If you are not, you can get started with my other book, *DuckDB Database: Learning SQL in CLI Client.*

Chapter 1: What is JSON?

JSON (JavaScript Object Notation) is an open standard **format** for **text-based** data. Binary data (such as multimedia) is not supported.

Format of JSON Text

A JSON text is a sequence of tokens, which includes: left and right square braces, left and right curly braces; number, string, null, true, and false.

The following twelve records, stored in a text file named example.json, comply to JSON format. You can create them using any text editor of your choice.

```
111
-22
3.33
-44.4
"HR"
false
true
null
[1, 60, false, "available", "part-time", null]
{"age": 71, "retired":true, "date": "2000-01-31"}
{"name": "Herb Sims", "skills":["SQL", "JSON"]}
["children", {"girls": ["Ann","Berth"], "boys": [null]
      }]
```

In DuckDB, you can use the JSON_VALID function to check if a text is JSON or not. If the function returns a true then the text complies to the format, it is a valid JSON data; false if is not a valid JSON data; and null if the JSON data is null.

The following query with the JSON_VALID function returns true to all data, except null, which as expected, returns null. Note that json is the column name, by default, returned by the query.

```
SELECT *, JSON_VALID(json) AS type FROM
    'example.json';
```

```
D SELECT *, JSON_VALID(json) AS type FROM 'example.json';
```

json json	type boolean
111	true
-22	true
3.33	true
-44.4	true
"HR"	true
false	true
true	true
[1,60,false,"available","part-time",null]	true
{"age":71,"retired":true,"date":"2000-01-31"}	true
{"name":"Herb Sims","skills":["SQL","JSON"]}	true
["children",{"girls":["Ann","Berth"],"boys":[null]}]	true

```
12 rows                                              2 columns
```

JSON Types

Let's find out the JSON type of our twelve data by applying
JSON_TYPE function as shown in the query below.

```
SELECT *, JSON_TYPE(json) AS type FROM 'example.json';
```

Before you run the query, please run .nullvalue NULL as
shown in the following screenshot, so that null will be
displayed as NULL; otherwise, null will display nothing (blank)

```
D .nullvalue NULL
D
D SELECT *, JSON_TYPE(json) AS type FROM 'example.json';

                            json                        type
                            json                        varchar

 111                                                    UBIGINT
 -22                                                    BIGINT
 3.33                                                   DOUBLE
 -44.4                                                  DOUBLE
 "HR"                                                   VARCHAR
 false                                                  BOOLEAN
 true                                                   BOOLEAN
 NULL                                                   NULL
 [1,60,false,"available","part-time",null]              ARRAY
 {"age":71,"retired":true,"date":"2000-01-31"}          OBJECT
 {"name":"Herb Sims","skills":["SQL","JSON"]}           OBJECT
 ["children",{"girls":["Ann","Berth"], "boys":[null]}]  ARRAY

 12 rows                                                2 columns
```

As you can see on the result, the JSON types are:

- UBIGINT, BIGINT, or DOUBLE, for numbers
- VARCHAR for string, which must be enclosed in
  double quotes
- BOOLEAN for true or false, which must be in **lower
  cases**
- null for null, which must be in **lower case**
- ARRAY, with elements separated by comma and can
  be mixed types, and must be enclosed in square braces
- OBJECT, with members in the form of name:value
  pairs, must be enclosed in curly braces; also, name and
  value must be separated by a colon, and members are
  separated by a comma.

8

Nesting

The last member of the object {"name":"Herb Sims","skills":**["SQL","JSON"]**} has an array as its value; we say, it is a nested array.

The last element of the array ["children",**{"girls":["Ann","Berth"],"boys":null}**] is a nested object, and its member "girls":["Ann","Berth"] is a nested array.

Loading JSON into a SQL Table

Let's create a table, named **example** with a JSON column named **js,** and load the example.json file.

```
CREATE TABLE example (js JSON);
INSERT INTO example (SELECT * FROM 'example.json');
```

Let's check to confirm that the twelve rows were indeed correctly.

```
SELECT * FROM example;
```

```
D CREATE TABLE example (js JSON);
D INSERT INTO example (SELECT * FROM 'example.json');
D SELECT * FROM example;
```

js
json
111
-22
3.33
-44.4
"HR"
false
true
NULL
[1,60,false,"available","part-time",null]
{"age":71,"retired":true,"date":"2000-01-31"}
{"name":"Herb Sims","skills":["SQL","JSON"]}
["children",{"girls":["Ann","Berth"],"boys":[null]}]
12 rows

Creating JSON from a column with JSON datatype

You can create a JSON file from rows with only a column with JSON datatype.

The following COPY statement creates ex.json file from the example table that we earlier created and populated with the twelve JSON data.

```
COPY (SELECT * FROM example) TO 'ex.json';
```

You can confirm the JSON file contains the twelve records by querying directly the ex.json file:

```
SELECT * FROM 'ex.json';
```

```
D SELECT * FROM 'ex.json';
```

js
json
111
-22
3.33
-44.4
"HR"
false
true
NULL
[1,60,false,"available","part-time",null]
{"age":71,"retired":true,"date":"2000-01-31"}
{"name":"Herb Sims","skills":["SQL","JSON"]}
["children",{"girls":["Ann","Berth"],"boys":[null]}]

```
12 rows
```

Creating JSON From SQL Columns

JSON data is generally generated by serializing structured data.

Assume we have the following exm table with four columns populated with two rows:

```
CREATE TABLE exm (id INT, name VARCHAR, dob DATE,
     retired BOOLEAN);
INSERT INTO exm VALUES(1,'Brad Pizz','1960-01-01',
     true), (2,'Beau Angel','1990-12-31',false);
```

The following COPY statement creates an exm.json file:

```
COPY exm TO 'exm.json';
```

When you the open the exm.json file, you will see two json records; they're the generated json objects serialized from the exm's columns.

```
{"id":1,"name":"Brad Pizz","dob":"1960-01-
    01","retired":true}
{"id":2,"name":"Beau Angel","dob":"1990-12-
    31","retired":false}
```

You can load the json file into table. The following example loads only three columns out of four from exm.json file into the e table.

```
CREATE TABLE e(id INT, name TEXT, dob DATE);
INSERT INTO e (SELECT id, name, dob FROM 'exm.json');

SELECT * FROM e;
```

Now that you know what JSON is, you will, in the next chapters, learn the JSON functions available in DuckDB.

Each of the next five chapters covers each of the six categories of the functions: Table, Scalar, Extraction, Creation, Aggregation, and Transformation.

Chapter 2: JSON File Functions

You will learn in this chapter functions that read json data from a text file.

READ_JSON_OBJECTS(filename)

The examples below use a pay.json file that has the following three records.

```
{"id":  200,"name":"Singh","staff":false,"pay":null}
{"id":300,"name":"Bears","staff":true,"pay":123456.78}
{"id":400,"name":"Kootz","staff":null,
    "pay":200000.01}
```

The default FORMAT parameter of the READ_JSON_OBJECTS function is ARRAY. As our json data in the pay.json file is not ARRAY, we need to specify the FORMAT = AUTO.

```
SELECT * FROM READ_JSON_OBJECTS('pay.json',
    FORMAT=AUTO);
```

```
D SELECT * FROM READ_JSON_OBJECTS('pay.json', FORMAT=AUTO);
┌─────────────────────────────────────────────────────────┐
│                          json                             │
│                          json                             │
├─────────────────────────────────────────────────────────┤
│ {"id":  200,"name":"Singh","staff":false,"pay":null}      │
│ {"id":300,"name":"Bears","staff":true,"pay":123456.78}    │
│ {"id":400,"name":"Kootz","staff":null, "pay":200000.01}   │
└─────────────────────────────────────────────────────────┘
```

The following example inserts the json data into pay table.

```
CREATE TABLE pay(js JSON);
```

```
INSERT INTO pay (SELECT * FROM
    READ_JSON_OBJECTS('pay.json', FORMAT=AUTO));
```

The following query confirms the pay table has the rows as expected:

```
D SELECT * FROM pay;
```

js json
{"id": 200,"name":"Singh","staff":false,"pay":null}
{"id":300,"rame":"Bears","staff":true,"pay":123456.78}
{"id":400,"name":"Kootz","staff":null, "pay":200000.01}

Multiple Files

Let's say we have another file p.json that has the following two records:

```
{"id":   200,"name":"Sam","staff":false,"pay":null}
{"id":300,"name":"Bo","staff":true,"pay":123456.78}
```

You can uses the same function to read both files by listing them (put them as elements of a list) as shown below:

```
SELECT * FRCM READ_JSON_OBJECTS(([ 'pay.json',
       'pa.json']), FORMAT=AUTO);
```

You will see all five rows returned by the following query:

```
SELECT * FROM READ_JSON_OBJECTS(([ 'pay.json',
       'pa.json']), FORMAT=AUTO);
```

```
D SELECT * FROM READ_JSON_OBJECTS(['pay.json', 'pa.json']), FORMAT=AUTO);
```

json json
{"id": 200,"name":"Singh","staff":false,"pay":null}
{"id":300,"name":"Bears","staff":true,"pay":123456.78}
{"id":400,"name":"Kootz","staff":null, "pay":200000.01}
{"id": 200,"name":"Sam","staff":false,"pay":null}
{"id":300,"name":"Bo","staff":true,"pay":123456.78}
{"id":400,"name":"Ken","staff":null, "pay":200000.01}

READ_JSON_OBJECTS_AUTO(filename e)

With this function, you don't need to specify FORMAT = AUTO.

The following query produces the same result as the previous one.

```
SELECT * FROM READ_JSON_OBJECTS_AUTO('pay.json');
```

```
D SELECT * FROM READ_JSON_OBJECTS_AUTO('pay.json');

                        json
                        json

{"id":   200,"name":"Singh","staff":false,"pay":null}
{"id":300,"name":"Bears","staff":true,"pay":123456.78}
{"id":400,"name":"Kootz","staff":null, "pay":200000.01}
```

Similar to the READ_JSON_OBJECTS function you can query **multiple files** with this function and also the next function.

READ_NDJSON_OBJECTS(filename)

The ND in NDJSON part of the name stands for Newline Delimited.

As our pay.json file is newline delimited, you can actually use this function, which will give you the same output as the previous examples.

```
SELECT * FROM READ_NDJSON_OBJECTS('pay.json');
```

```
D SELECT * FROM READ_NDJSON_OBJECTS('pay.json');
```

| json |
| json |
| {"id": 200,'name':"Singh","staff":false,"pay":null} |
| {"id":300,"name":"Bears","staff":true,"pay":123456.78} |
| {"id":400,"name":"Kootz","staff":null, "pay":200000.01} |

READ_JSON(filename)

While the READ_JSON_OBJECTS function reads json objects in a file, a READ_JSON function reads a file as if the file is a SQL table such that you can read specific columns only. Columns come from members of the objects in the json file.

Here is an example where only name and pay are read:

```
SELECT * FRCM READ_JSON('pay.json', COLUMNS =
    {name:'TEXT', pay:'DOUBLE'},
    FORMAT='newline_delimited');
```

Chapter 3: JSON Scalar Functions

Suppose you have the following JSON objects stored in a pay.json file.

```
{"id":  200,"name":"Singh","staff":false,"pay":null}
{"id":300,"name":"Bears","staff":true,"pay":123456.78}
{"id":400,"name":"Kootz","staff":null,
      "pay":200000.01}
```

And, load the following the JSON objects the js column of table pay.

```
CREATE TABLE pay (js VARCHAR);

COPY pay FROM 'pay.json' (FORMAT 'CSV', QUOTE '',
      DELIMITER '');
```

JSON(json)

JSON(**json**) function removes unnecessary white spaces from the text of the **json** parameter.

Here's a query without the JSON function. In the query result you can see that that there are white spaces in two places: "id": 200 (at the beginning of the first row) and in , "pay":200000.01 (at the end of the third row)

```
SELECT * FROM pay;
```

```
D SELECT * FROM pay;

                              js
                            varchar

{"id":  200,"name":"Singh","staff":false,"pay":null}
{"id":300,"name":"Bears","staff":true,"pay":123456.78}
{"id":400,"name":"Kootz","staff":null, "pay":200000.01}
```

And, here's a query with the JSON function:

```
SELECT JSON(js) FROM pay;
```

```
D SELECT JSON(js) FROM pay;
```

json(js) json
{"id":200,'name":"Singh","staff":false,"pay":null}
{"id":300,'name":"Bears","staff":true,"pay":123456.78}
{"id":400,'name":"Kootz","staff":null,"pay":200000.01}

If you compare the result of query with the JSON(json) function to the one without, you will see that the white spaces are removed.

JSON_VALID(json)

JSON_VALID(json) function validate the text in the json parameter; if the text is a well formatted JSON (valid JSON) then the function returns **true**, otherwise false.

```
SELECT JSON_VALID(js) FROM pay;
```

```
D SELECT JSON_VALID(js) FROM pay;
```

json_valid(js) boolean
true
true
true

Let's load the following three objects from pay_invalid.json file into the pay table.

Notice that these three are not valid JSON objects: the first
record is not enclosed in curly braces; the second, the name key
is not a valid JSON string as it does not have a closing double
quote; the third, the value "House" is not separated by a colon
from its key.

```
"id":999,"name":"Hogan","staff":null,  "pay":190000
{"id":888,"name: "Yang","staff":false,  "pay":180000}
{"id":777,"name" "House","staff":null,  "pay":120000}
```

```
COPY pay FROM 'pay_invalid.json' (FORMAT 'CSV', QUOTE '',
        DELIMITER '');
```

The pay table now has six rows.

```
SELECT * FROM pay;
```

```
D SELECT * FROM pay;
┌─────────────────────────────────────────────────────────┐
│                            js                             │
│                          varchar                          │
├─────────────────────────────────────────────────────────┤
│ {"id":   200,"name":"Singh","staff":false,"pay":null}     │
│ {"id":300,"name":"Bears","staff":true,"pay":123456.78}    │
│ {"id":400,"name":"Kootz","staff":null,  "pay":200000.01}  │
│ "id":999,"name":"Hogan","staff":null,  "pay":190000       │
│ {"id":888,"name: "Yang","staff":false,  "pay":180000}     │
│ {"id":777,"name" "House","staff":null,  "pay":120000}     │
└─────────────────────────────────────────────────────────┘
```

When we apply the JSON_VALID function, the last three
rows return false as expected.

```
SELECT JSON_VALID(js) FROM pay;
```

```
D SELECT JSON_VALID(js) FROM pay;

json_valid(js)
    boolean

true
true
true
false
false
false
```

JSON_TYPE(json [, path])

The JSON_TYPE can have an optional path parameter. A
path is a text enclosed in single quotes. The text starts with a $
(dollar sign) followed by a . (dot) and then a key of the json
parameter which is an object. But, if the json parameter is an
array then the dot is followed by the index in square braces
[index].

Please delete all rows in the pay table, and load the following
JSON objects into the pay table.

```
{"id":789,"name":"Herb","staff":true,"pay":100000.99}
{"id":123,"name":{"1st":"Ann","last":"Ho"},"staff":tru
     e,"pay":null}
{"id":-
     456,"name":["Nora","Fans"],"staff":true,"pay":nu
     ll}
```

Run the following query to find out the JSON types of the
values of the keys directed by the paths. For example, to find
the type of value of the id key, the path parameter is '$.id'.

```
SELECT JSON_TYPE(js,'$.id') idtyp,
JSON_TYPE(js, '$.name') nametyp,
```

```
JSON_TYPE(js,'$.staff') stafftyp,
JSON_TYPE(js,'$.pay') paytyp
FROM pay;
```

```
D SELECT JSON_TYPE(js,'$.id') idtyp,
> JSON_TYPE(js, '$.name') nametyp,
> JSON_TYPE(js,'$.staff') stafftyp,
> JSON_TYPE(js,'$.pay') paytyp
> FROM pay;
```

idtyp varchar	nametyp varchar	stafftyp varchar	paytyp varchar
UBIGINT	VARCHAR	BOOLEAN	DOUBLE
UBIGINT	OBJECT	BOOLEAN	NULL
BIGINT	ARRAY	BOOLEAN	NULL

The JSON type of the value of the name key of the 2nd row is OBJECT; and the 3rd row is ARRAY. They are a nested object and a nested array, respectively.

To find out the type of the a nested object value or array element you have provided their paths down to the nested levels.

In the following query, for the select first column (alias arrtype) the JSON_TYPE's path points to the first element (index 0) of the name array. As the names of first two rows are not array, the result is NULL; the third row is an array and the JSON type of its **first element** is VARCHAR (string "Nora")

For the select second column (alias objtyp) the JSON_TYPE's path points to the first element (index 0) of the name object. As the names of first and third rows are not object, the result is NULL; the second row is an object and the JSON type of its key **1st** is VARCHAR (string "Ann")

```
SELECT JSON_TYPE(js,'$.name[0]') arrtyp,
JSON_TYPE(js,'$.name.1st') objtyp
FROM pay;
```

```
D SELECT JSON_TYPE(js,'$.name[0]') arrtyp,
> JSON_TYPE(js,'$.name.1st') objtyp
> FROM pay;
```

arrtyp varchar	objtyp varchar
NULL	NULL
NULL	VARCHAR
VARCHAR	NULL

JSON_ARRAY_LENGTH(json [, path])

This function returns the number of elements of the array in the json text as pointed by its path parameter. If it's not an array, the returned value is 0.

The following query applies the function on the pay table used previously. As the name of the first two rows are not array, as you see when you run the query, the result is 0. The last row has its **name** array with two elements "name":[**"Nora","Fans"**], hence the result is 2.

```
SELECT JSON_ARRAY_LENGTH(js,'$.name') arrtyp FROM pay;
```

```
D SELECT JSON_ARRAY_LENGTH(js,'$.name') arrtyp FROM pay;
```

arrtyp uint64
0
0
2

JSON_KEYS(json [,path])

JSON_KEYS returns the keys of json if json is a JSON object. The keys are returned as a SQL list. If json is not a JSON object, the returned list is empty. The optional path directs to the target object.

The JSON_KEYS function in the following query does not specify a path, hence the function returns all four keys from the js object.

```
SELECT JSON_KEYS(js) arrtyp FROM pay;
```

```
D SELECT JSON_KEYS(js) arrtyp FROM pay;

            arrtyp
           varchar[]

 [id, name, staff, pay]
 [id, name, staff, pay]
 [id, name, staff, pay]
```

If you specify a path as in the following query, as the name path is specified as object ($. followed by key) and only the second row has an object as the value, the function on the other rows returns empty lists.

```
SELECT JSON_KEYS(js,'$.name') keys FROM pay;
```

```
D SELECT JSON_KEYS(js,'$.name') keys FROM pay;

     keys
   varchar[]

 []
 [1st, last]
 []
```

JSON_STRUCTURE(json)

This function returns the structure of json text parameter.

Essentially a structure is JSON type as you can see in the following example. The whole row is an object as it's enclosed in curly braces. The object has four key value pairs. Type of values are shown, in place of the actual values.

```
SELECT JSON_STRUCTURE(js) AS struct
FROM pay;
```

```
D SELECT JSON_STRUCTURE(js) AS struct  FROM pay;
┌─────────────────────────────────────────────────────────────────────────────────────┐
│                                        struct                                         │
│                                         json                                          │
├───────────────────────────────────────────────────────────────────────────────────────┤
│ {"id":"UBIGINT","name":"VARCHAR","staff":"BOOLEAN","pay":"DOUBLE"}                     │
│ {"id":"UBIGINT","name":{"1st":"VARCHAR","last":"VARCHAR"},"staff":"BOOLEAN","pay":"NULL"} │
│ {"id":"BIGINT","name":["VARCHAR"],"staff":"BOOLEAN","pay":"NULL"}                      │
└─────────────────────────────────────────────────────────────────────────────────────┘
```

The return value is "JSON" if json is an array and the type of its elements are not consistent, as demonstrated in the following example.

```
SELECT JSON_STRUCTURE('[1,"a"]') AS inconsistent_type;
```

```
D SELECT JSON_STRUCTURE('[1,"a"]') AS inconsistent_type;
┌───────────────────────┐
│   inconsistent_type   │
│         json          │
├───────────────────────┤
│ ["JSON"]              │
└───────────────────────┘
```

If the parameter is not a valid json, the query will be erroneous, as exemplified in the following example where the array does not have a closing square bracket.

```
SELECT JSON_STRUCTURE('[1,"a"');
```

```
D SELECT JSON_STRUCTURE('[1,"a"');
Error: Invalid Input Error: Malformed JSON at byte 6 of input:
 unexpected end of data.   Input: [1,"a"
```

JSON_CONTAINS(json, searchvalue)

Use this function to search a json text for a value. If the value is found in the json text, true is returned; otherwise, false.

The following query for example returns true as a value 123 is in the second row of the pay table; false on the other two rows.

```
SELECT JSON_CONTAINS(js, 123) FROM pay;
```

```
D SELECT JSON_CONTAINS(js, 123) FROM pay;

  json_contains(js, 123)
          boolean

  false
  true
  false
```

As "Ho" exists on the second row as the value of key **last**, the second row returns true,, the other rows returns false.

```
SELECT JSON_CONTAINS(js, '"Ho"') FROM pay;
```

```
D SELECT JSON_CONTAINS(js, '"Ho"') FROM pay;

 json_contains(js, '"Ho"')
          boolean

 false
 true
 false
```

"Nora" is the first element of the array value in the third row, hence this row returns a true; the other rows as they don't have the searchvalue return false.

```
SELECT JSON_CONTAINS(js, '"Nora"') FROM pay;
```

```
D SELECT JSON_CONTAINS(js, '"Nora"') FROM pay;

 json_contains(js, '"Nora"')
          boolean

 false
 false
 true
```

That's all the scalar functions. In the next chapter, you will learn JSON Extraction functions.

Chapter 4: JSON Extraction Functions

JSON_EXTRACT(json, path)

This function returns the object value(s) at the path. The path parameter is mandatory.

The following query uses JSON_EXTRACT function with a variety of path.

```
SELECT JSON_EXTRACT(js,'$.name') nm,
JSON_EXTRACT(js,'$.name[1]') arr,
JSON_EXTRACT(js,'$.name.last') obj,
JSON_EXTRACT(js, '$.pay') pay
FROM pay;
```

```
D SELECT JSON_EXTRACT(js,'$.name') nm,
> JSON_EXTRACT(js,'$.name[1]') arr,
> JSON_EXTRACT(js,'$.name.last') obj,
> JSON_EXTRACT(js, '$.pay') pay
> FROM pay;
```

nm json	arr json	obj json	pay json
"Herb"	NULL	NULL	100000.99
{"1st":"Ann","last":"Ho"}	NULL	"Ho"	NULL
["Nora","Fans"]	"Fans"	NULL	NULL

Extraction Operator

Instead of path, you can use an extraction operator ->

In the same query as above, instead of JSON_EXTRACT functions, extraction operators are used in the query below. The result is the same.

28

```
SELECT (js ->'$.name') nm,
(js ->'$.name[1]') arr,
(js->'$.name.last') obj,
(js -> '$.pay') pay
FROM pay;
```

```
D SELECT (js ->'$.name') nm,
> (js ->'$.name[1]') arr,
> (js->'$.name.last') obj,
> (js -> '$.pay') pay
> FROM pay;
```

nm json	arr json	obj json	pay json
"Herb"	NULL	NULL	100000.99
{"1st":"Ann","last":"Ho"}	NULL	"Ho"	NULL
["Nora","Fans"]	"Fans"	NULL	NULL

JSON_EXTRACT_STRING(json, path)

While JSON_EXTRACT produces JSON string (the double quotes), JSON_EXTRACT_STRING produces SQL string; for example, instead of "Herb", you now get Herb.

```
SELECT JSON_EXTRACT_STRING(js,'$.name') nm,
JSON_EXTRACT_STRING(js,'$.name[1]') arr,
JSON_EXTRACT_STRING(js,'$.name.last') obj,
JSON_EXTRACT_STRING(js, '$.pay') pay
FROM pay;
```

```
D SELECT JSON_EXTRACT_STRING(js,'$.name') nm,
> JSON_EXTRACT_STRING(js,'$.name[1]') arr,
> JSON_EXTRACT_STRING(js,'$.name.last') obj,
> JSON_EXTRACT_STRING(js, '$.pay') pay
> FROM pay;
```

nm varchar	arr varchar	obj varchar	pay varchar
Herb	NULL	NULL	100000.99
{"1st":"Ann","last":"Ho"}	NULL	Ho	NULL
["Nora","Fans"]	Fans	NULL	NULL

SQL String Extraction Operator

You can use extraction operator ->> instead of the JSON_EXTRACTION_STRING function. The result will be the same as shown below.

```
SELECT (js ->>'$.name') nm,
(js ->>'$.name[1]') arr,
(js->>'$.name.last') obj,
(js ->> '$.pay') pay
FROM pay;
```

```
D SELECT (js ->>'$.name') nm,
> (js ->>'$.name[1]') arr,
> (js->>'$.name.last') obj,
> (js ->> '$.pay') pay
> FROM pay;
```

nm varchar	arr varchar	obj varchar	pay varchar
Herb	NULL	NULL	100000.99
{"1st":"Ann","last":"Ho"}	NULL	Ho	NULL
["Nora","Fans"]	Fans	NULL	NULL

Chapter 5: JSON Creation Functions

The five JSON creation functions you will learn in this chapter return (create) JSON objects.

TO_JSON or JSON_QUOTE

JSON_QUOTE and its alias TO_JSON create JSON of any type.

Let's look at the following example.

Table toy has four columns, with data types INT, TEXT, LIST and STRUCTURE, respectively.

```
CREATE TABLE toy
(id iNT, name TEXT, type VARCHAR[],
item STRUCT(i VARCHAR, price REAL));
```

Let's insert a row:

```
INSERT INTO toy VALUES(11, 'Hot Wheels', ['L','M'],
     ROW('Tow Truck', 99));
```

The following query uses TO_JSON and its alias JSON_QUOTE to get the JSON integer and varchar. As you can see on the result of the query, the two functions produces the same result.

```
SELECT
     TO_JSON(id),JSON_QUOTE(id),TO_JSON(name),JSON_QU
     OTE(name) FROM toy;
```

```
D SELECT TO_JSON(id),JSON_QUOTE(id),TO_JSON(name),JSON_QUOTE(name) FROM toy;
```

to_json(id) json	json_quote(id) json	to_json("name") json	json_quote("name") json
11	11	"Hot Wheels"	"Hot Wheels"

TO_JSON can also convert SQL list to JSON array, and SQL structure to JSON object.

```
SELECT TO_JSON(type), TO_JSON(item) FROM toy;
```

```
D SELECT TO_JSON(type), TO_JSON(item) FROM toy;
```

to_json("type") json	to_json(item) json
["L","M"]	{"i":"Tow Truck","price":99.0}

ARRAY_TO_JSON and ROW_JSON_QUOTE

You can also use ARRAY_TO_JSON to convert SQL list to JSON array, and ROW_TO_JSON to convert SQL structure to JSON object.

As you can see in the following example, the result is the same as in the previous example using the TO_JSON function.

```
SELECT ARRAY_TO_JSON(type), ROW_TO_JSON(item) FROM
    toy;
```

```
D SELECT ARRAY_TO_JSON(type), ROW_TO_JSON(item) FROM toy;
```

array_to_json("type") json	row_to_json(item) json
["L","M"]	{"i":"Tow Truck","price":99.0}

JSON_OBJECT(key1,value1, key2, value2, ...)

Using JSON_OBJECT you can create a JSON object with as many key value pairs as you want.

```
SELECT JSON_CBJECT('id',101,'name','Abe','degrees',
['BA','MPH','PHD']) obj;
```

```
D SELECT JSON_OBJECT('id',101,'name','Abe','degrees',
> ['BA','MPH','PHD']) obj;
```

obj json
{"id":101,"rame":"Abe","degrees":["BA","MPH","PHD"]}

You must provide an even number of parameters that form JSON objects, otherwise the function will be erroneous.

```
SELECT JSON_OBJECT('id',101,'name','Abe','degrees');
```

```
D SELECT JSON_OBJECT('id',101,'name','Abe','degrees');
Error: Invalid Input Error: json object() requires an even number of arguments
```

JSON_MERGE_PATCH(json1, json2)

This function merges two or more JSON objects into one object.

As you can see in the result, the merging is from the right most object to its left's.

```
SELECT JSON_MERGE_PATCH('{"id":101}',
'{"name":"Abe"}', '{"children":2}');
```

```
D SELECT JSON_MERGE_PATCH('{"id":101}',
> '{"name":"Abe"}', '{"children":2}');

json_merge_patch('{"id":101}', '{"name":"Abe"}', '{"children":2}')
                              json

{"children":2,"name":"Abe","id":101}
```

Chapter 6: JSON Aggregation Functions

In this chapter you will learn the three JSON aggregation functions.

JSON_GROUP_ARRAY(any)

This function, which takes only one parameter of any data, creates a **JSON array** with one or more elements. Elements are from the aggregation of the parameter. The parameter can be of **any** data type.

Suppose we have the following agg table.

```
CREATE TABLE agg(k TEXT, v DOUBLE, i INT, ls
      VARCHAR[]);
```

With two rows:

```
INSERT INTO agg VALUES('price',123.44, 99, ['Abe',
      40]),
('discount',4567, 987.06, ['Bust',50]);
```

You can create a JSON array from any of the columns.

The following query creates a JSON array with elements from v column, which is a **numeric** double data type.

```
SELECT JSON_GROUP_ARRAY(v) FROM agg;
```

```
D SELECT JSON_GROUP_ARRAY(v) FROM agg;

  json_group_array(v)
         json

  [123.44,4567.0]
```

Next is an example of creating a JSON array from the ls column, the data type of which is list, hence the query returns a JSON array with **array** elements.

```
SELECT JSON_GROUP_ARRAY(ls) FROM agg;
```

```
D SELECT JSON_GROUP_ARRAY(ls) FROM agg;

        json_group_array(ls)
               json

  [["Abe","40"],["Bust","50"]]
```

JSON_GROUP_OBJECT(key,value)

Use this function to create a JSON object from the two parameters, which must be a string for the key, the value can be any data valid for JSON value.

Using the same table used in the previous example, the following query creates a JSON object the function's parameter, the k and v columns.

```
SELECT JSON_GROUP_OBJECT(k, v) FROM agg;
```

```
D SELECT JSON_GROUP_OBJECT(k, v) FROM agg;
```

json_group_object(k, v)
json
{"price":123.44,"discount":4567.0}

JSON_STRUCTURE(json)

This function shows you the structure of the json structure of the json text in the parameter. A structure is in the format, "key":json_type.

For the example, we'll use the js column of the pay table, as shown below.

```
SELECT * FROM pay;
```

```
D SELECT * FROM pay;

                                        js
                                      varchar

{"id":789,"name":"Herb","staff":true,"pay":100000.99}
{"id":123,"name":{"1st":"Ann","last":"Ho"},"staff":true,"pay":null}
{"id":-456,"name":["Nora","Fans"],"staff":true,"pay":null}
```

The query below uses the JSON_STRUCTURE function. The result for example shows the JSON structure of the first row are "id" key with UBIGINT type for its value; "name" with VARCHAR, and so on for its next columns. The second row shows the "name" key has a value of an object; while the third row, for the same key, its value is an array of VARCHAR.

```
SELECT JSON_STRUCTURE(js) FROM pay;
```

```
D SELECT JSON_STRUCTURE(js) FROM pay;

                                  json_structure(js)
                                        json

{"id":"UBIGINT","name":"VARCHAR","staff":"BOOLEAN","pay":"DOUBLE"}
{"id":"UBIGINT","name":{"1st":"VARCHAR","last":"VARCHAR"},"staff":"BOOLEAN","pay":"NULL"}
{"id":"BIGINT","name":["VARCHAR"],"staff":"BOOLEAN","pay":"NULL"}
```

Chapter 7: JSON Transforming Functions

Two JSON transforming functions are provided; their difference is on how they handle errors.

JSON_TRANSFORM(json, structure)

Using this function, you can transform (modify) using the JSON parameter, json data into the desired structure by specifying it in the parameter.

Suppose a *transform* table has the following three rows of objects. Notice members of these objects are not exactly the same; for example, the first object has a "contract": "expiring" member, the second and third records do not.

```
CREATE TABLE transform(js JSON);
INSERT INTO transform VALUES(
'{"id":  200,"name":"Singh","staff":false,"pay":null, "contract":
       "expiring"}'),
('{"id":300,"name":"Bears","staff":true,"pay":123456.78, "bonus %":
       10}'),
('{"id":400,"name":"Kootz","staff":null, "pay":200000.01}')
;
```

Using the JSON_TRANSFORM function you can for example query all records specifying a structure in the function's parameter such that the result will have only "name" and "contract" members.

```
SELECT
json_transform(js, '{"name": "TEXT", "contract":
     "TEXT"}')
FROM transform;
```

As you can see on the output below, those rows that do not have "contract" member will be returned with "contract" members, but the values are of course NULL, these last two rows returned by the query have their members transformed (modified).

```
D SELECT
> json_transform(js, '{"name": "TEXT", "contract": "TEXT"}')
> FROM transform;

json_transform(js, '{"name": "TEXT", "contract": "TEXT"}')
          struct("name" varchar, contract varchar)

{'name': Singh, 'contract': expiring}
{'name': Bears, 'contract': NULL}
{'name': Kootz, 'contract': NULL}
```

JSON_TRANSFORM_STRICT(json, structure)

While the JSON_TRANSFORM function takes an incorrect data type in the structure parameter, this function strictly rejects, the query will fail.

Let's compare the two functions.

Notice that the "name" value should have a "TEXT" type, but it is "BOOLEAN" in the JSON_TRANSFORM parameter. They are NULL on the returned rows. The query does not fail.

```
SELECT JSON_TRANSFORM(js, '{"name": "BOOLEAN",
       "contract": "TEXT"}')  FROM transform;
```

```
D SELECT json_transform(js, '{"name": "BOOLEAN", "contract": "TEXT"}') FROM transform;

json_transform(js, '{"name": "BOOLEAN", "contract": "TEXT"}')
          struct("name" boolean, contract varchar)

{'name': NULL, 'contract': expiring}
{'name': NULL, 'contract': NULL}
{'name': NULL, 'contract': NULL}
```

The next query uses JSON_TRANSFORM_STRICT. It fails due to the "INT" type, which should be "TEXT".

```
SELECT JSON_TRANSFORM_STRICT
(js,'{"name":"INT","contract":"TEXT"}')
FROM transform;
```

```
D SELECT JSON_TRANSFORM_STRICT
> (js,'{"name":"INT","contract":"TEXT"}')
> FROM transform;
Error: Invalid Input Error: Failed to cast value to numerical: "Kootz"
```

Appendix A: Getting Started with DuckDB and CLI (Command Line Interface)

This chapter guides you how to download DuckDB with CLI and install it.

Downloading

Download CLI from
https://duckdb.org/docs/installation/index

Select the installation zip file for your platform. In my case I selected the first one, Linux 64-bit.

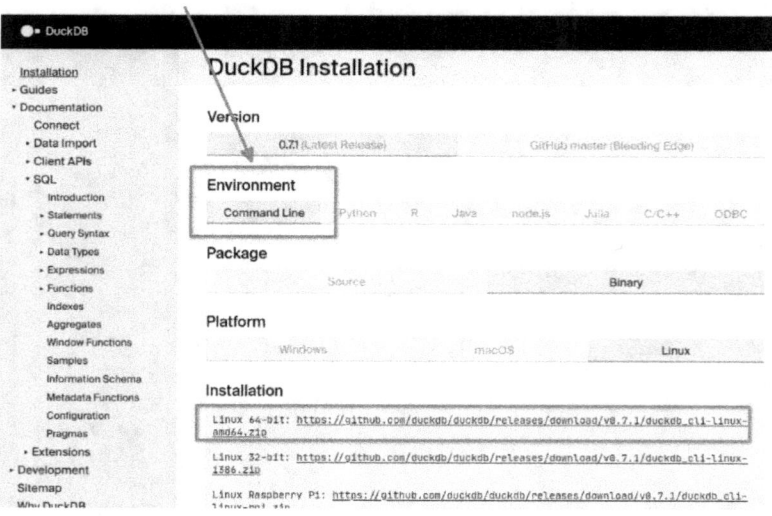

Installing

Extract the downloaded zip file into a folder of your choice.

When extraction is completed, under that folder a sub folder, something like duckdb_cli-linux-amd64 is created, where you see a file named **duckdb**.

You use this duckdb to run CLI , and then create a database and all its objects.

In my case, I extracted to CLI folder. So, in my Ubuntu terminal, I can see the duckdb like the following:

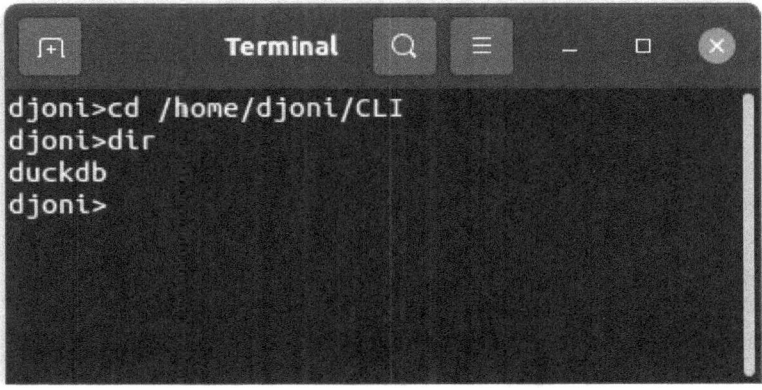

To start the duckdb CLI terminal, run the duckdb file as follows:

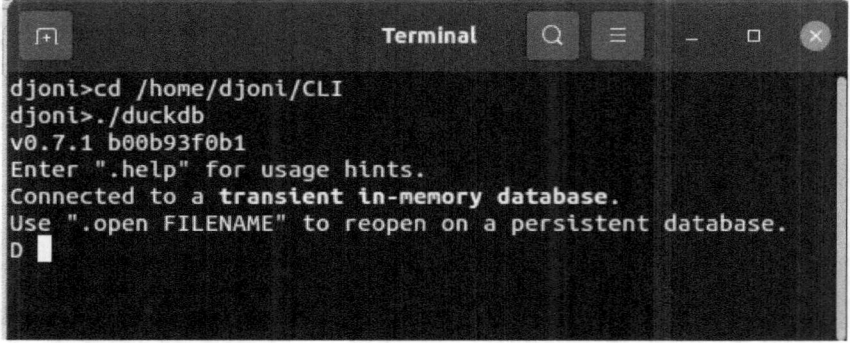

To create a new database, for example a database named book.duckdb, run the following. If the database already exists, it will be opened.

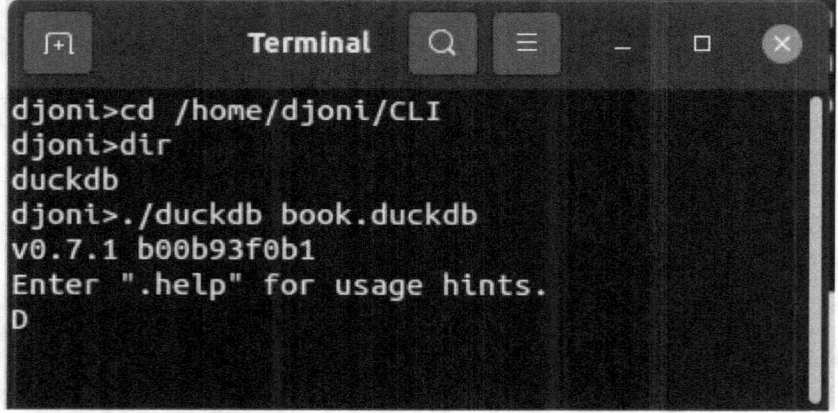

To exit DuckDB CLI, press ctrl + d. You will be back to your unix terminal.

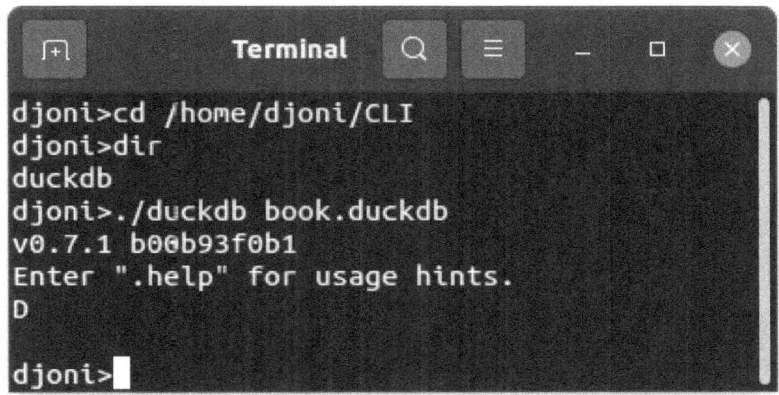

```
djoni>cd /home/djoni/CLI
djoni>dir
duckdb
djoni>./duckdb book.duckdb
v0.7.1 b00b93f0b1
Enter ".help" for usage hints.
D

djoni>
```

Now that you are in the DuckDB CLI, you can run SQL statement.

To start with, create a schema. Below I created a schema named **book_schema** in the **book** database. Don't forget to terminate your SQL with a semicolon.

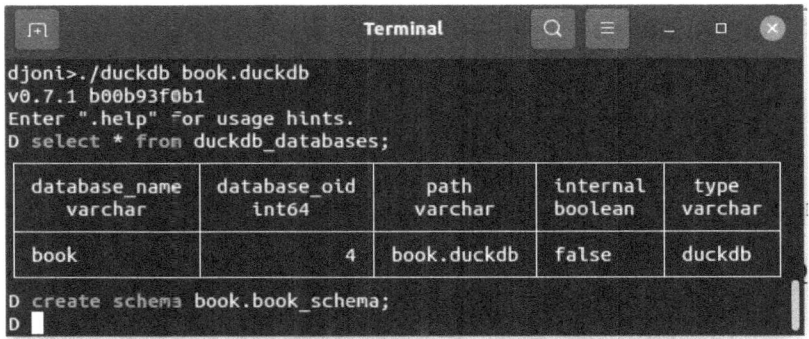

```
djoni>./duckdb book.duckdb
v0.7.1 b00b93f0b1
Enter ".help" for usage hints.
D select * from duckdb_databases;
```

database_name varchar	database_oid int64	path varchar	internal boolean	type varchar
book	4	book.duckdb	false	duckdb

```
D create schema book.book_schema;
D
```

You can display the schema by running a select * from duckdb_schemas statement as follows:

```
D create schema book_schema;
D select * from duckdb_schemas;
```

oid int64	database_name varchar	database_oid int64	schema_name varchar	internal boolean	sql varchar
1371	book	4	book_schema	false	

```
D
```

Next, let's create table named dummy with just one column, d of type integer. To confirm the table was created, you can query the duck_tables built in data dictionary's table duckdb_tables.

```
D create table dummy (d integer);
D select schema_name, table_name from duckdb_tables;
```

schema_name varchar	table_name varchar
main	dummy

The dummy table we just created is under the **main** schema. We actually wanted the table under our own schema, book_schema. We can do so by using a dot notation schemaname.tablename as follows.

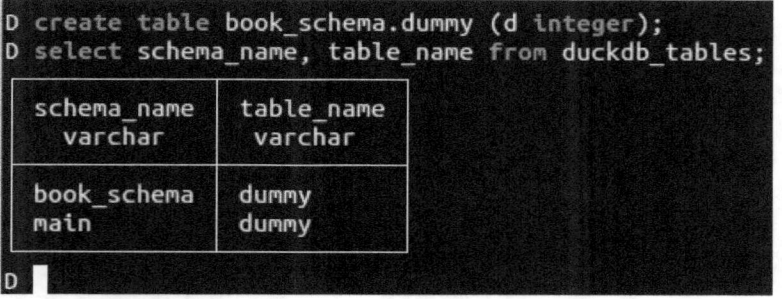

```
D create table book_schema.dummy (d integer);
D select schema_name, table_name from duckdb_tables;
```

schema_name varchar	table_name varchar
book_schema	dummy
main	dummy

```
D
```

If you will often work with the book_schema, rather than prefixing with the schema-name, you can set book_schema as a **default** schema. Then when you create a table that you want it under the default schema, you don't need to specify the schema.

Below we set book_schema as the default schema. Then, we create dummy2 table with out specifying any schema. The dummy2 is created under book_schema.

```
D set schema to book_schema;
D create table dummy2(d1 text);
D select schema_name, table_name from duckdb_tables;
```

schema_name varchar	table_name varchar
book_schema book_schema main	dummy2 dummy dummy

This is the end of the Appendix and the book.

Good luck with applying your JSON skill.